SHORT BLUES

by

Gabriel Posey

about: the title page

For more information, address: gabriel@gabrielposey.com.
First paperback edition January 2021

ISBN 978-0-5788-3700-0 (hardback) 9780578836997
ISBN 978-0-5788-3699-7 (ebook)

www.gabrielposey.com

about: this is my work, please don't steal it

Friends,

This work represents the months of September through December of 2020.

In that period of time I went through a sea change that sprouted from me like a rose from a pavement crack.

I thank God for that.

There is no dedication here, but you might spy a name in these pages you recognize. You might think of one of these as more about you than the person it's supposed to be about.

That's ok.

Take these morsels, eat, be full and happy.

Gabriel Posey
January 2021

about: the beginning of this little poetry book

it was such a sweet sound
doomed as is all life, that comes from that place
where we started

where the sparks
and the cosmic dust swirls

around us as we descended, like young kids
laughing
the whole way down

about: this is about the beginnings of marriage

do your colors sing?
do they lilt into ancient rafters?
do your songs, through voices old, rise?

I see you there, waiting
afraid to rise yourself
afraid to say what you really want
even in the dark
even to yourself

losing time is new for you
there is a much longer road ahead

about: getting lost in a hymn

i name you little feather
i see your gliding, your falling
your contentment not to fly
over the wastes of life

i name you little feather
never in a hand, never rested
but content to keep falling
in love

i name you little feather
and one day you will write,
in boldness
your song

about: sarah part two

you don't possess the future
nor do you wear it, a ring on your finger

but fear it, woe it, faint in light of it,
if you must
 but none will change it, twist it, nor

make it a threat
if you would but vote
and cast in ink that choice for your own joy

about: about finding your own joy

i fall up into the arms
of waiting innocence
be it now or in the hereafter

i'm out of charms
and excuses
that would absolve my filthy tears

until the unknown
whispers my real name

about: letting go of control, and seeing god

in a dream figured out a way
 to follow each other
 at the same time

 like young lovers
twirling and whirling
dancing barefoot
 on soft grass

somehow dancing our way
 towards a destiny of joy
 a place neither of us thought possible
 where the dancing goes on and on

about: what if part one

it was a chain
and when that part of town 'went to hell'
there just wasn't the clientele there anymore
but it was where i gave her that ruby necklace
and we ate our weight in table bread
and no matter if the food was terrible,
both for us, and experienced by us,
but it was us.

about: the prompt was about a restaurant closing down

it strikes when you least expect it
 not unlike the grinch with his heart
aburst
sneaking back into
those pillaged homes
to save what was lost
 to redeem what was broken
to bring
joy
 oh you subtle grinch, oh you sneaky messenger
oh you smile on the face of god

about: hope, part one

i pinned a stack of photos to my corkboard
of emotions
and thoughts
that started at 14 and
and
stayed
because, because that was there, that was where i heard
my voice
telling me these memories needed to stay there
and then i ripped one down
and crumplethrew it at you
but you
saw

about: the sobering terror of having revealed yourself

did you say `shh' when you blew the candles out
or did you watch the light recede towards
that little wick
until it was a nit of fire
swirling with ghosts of smoke

 did you say `shh' to my soul
and somehow
it still burns

about: peace

i'm fuel on fire and my smoke is
just
the
billows
of
joy

about: the joy of writing poetry in under 90 seconds

they say it's called crown shyness
when the tips of tree limbs refuse
 to meet

but the truth is
we're seeing their most
intimate of places
 breathing
deep

about: trees and breath

you think of it like wonder woman's lasso,
and that should tell you volumes
about what you really
really
want

about: connection

did they
give up
or was
that just the best they could do
because
it feels like a deep, awe-filled sigh
that moment of saying it's two and and it's one and it's two and it's...

...
selah
...

to even see the raging wonder of a God
to even attempt to encapsulate

selah

about: the Council of Chalcedon

i don't deserve the blues
i don't deserve the excuses for why not
i don't deserve the horns playing soft and low

for you

and not

for me

about: tension in wanting to move on, but needing to stay

there's a lack of noise
when you grasp a small
box of matches
and give them that expectant
shake
and then, there's nothing but
a box
in your hand
and a cold candle before you

about: light

oh sweet piano melody
in traces and paths worn deep by old shoes
drawing, like magician's scarves
but always scarlet
comes the sound
comes the call
the very sigh
of all life

about: laura who runs

i miss that moment when i'm just
on the very edge of a person for the first time
and our eyes dance across each other's
not wanting to dwell, because awkotacos,
but also then their scent wafts over and
you can tell how they do laundry
and what kind of body wash it is
and you see

about: missing connection to people because of covid

there's an inch
or is it half an inch?
between the perfection of riding into that blazing
western sky
with tacky button-down shirts of colors splashed that little inch
that half an inch of ORANGE
that...
that,
that stupid visor won't touch
and i guess i'm happy and blind.

about: the sun in your eyes on roadtrips

did you have needles when you knit me?
did it hurt, but you let me forget it?
your mercy
your comfort
to both make
 and remake
all for glory

about: healing

it's ice melting off a flower,
caught,
in that late meadow when the freeze blasted in and kept it,
as that ice of time slides off,
but before a new day has seized them,
weathered them, tired them,
there they are, the way they used to be.

about: the face of a sleeping child

in the infinite moments of grinding facets
into
the
steep faces
of a diamond,

there's always a

chance

it
shatters

about: uncertainty

we danced once
in the steerage deck
with glee and abandon

but it was actually our wedding night
and there would be no flood
no calamity
just the dark
and one
where it had been
two

about: marriage

sepia-hues of midwinter
swirl around you, drawing tussles from around your ears
 in playful, cold-breathed delights
muffled and rebuffed by that cable-knit sweater listening to black crows

while you feel your way back
(a whisper) back where you came
 from
(a whisper) back to

about: winter photos

oh god
it's lightning running liquid down to the smallest place of my back
and squirming only serves me
for a
second
because it's in my eye and i oh
i see but it's blurry and that
is just
now i have to run and scream a little

about: cold rain

the sum of the parts i was holding in cut up hands
was supposed to be something
it was supposed to be me
but
there were
missing pieces
when i started

about: wholeness

what do i do with you
i don't, no, know, i don't
because you're out there on that
limb of life and
i can't shimmy towards you
but i'm so caught in your tree
and it holds me
right now
and for the time being
and maybe something will change
and i

i

won't just be nothing
to you

about: crushes for Meagan

it was a dream
where i ran from black and white room to black and white room in
 a house that had too many hallways
and nothing was after me
but something was coming
and i wrenched door open
 after doOR
 OPEN
 to find you

 you

you aren't there
behind door
 after
 door

about: abandonment

i admire the blush
that rises in you
passion and fire and shame and confusion
swirl inside your bonfire
where you turn the lies bullies spat at you
into golden runnels and rivulets

about: laura of the loch

little fox smile
little wiles in the tall grass
you know who you are

with limp and laugh
with tears and giggles
your life
your road
have gone in circles

around the same field
through the same grass
and one day

one day
you will run again

about: katie

learned you like a favorite novel
paperback
spine soft and creased

curled edges of yellowed pages
it's safe, there, between your lines
beneath those dog-eared folds

black and forth
through my mind
you hold my hand

about: trish

every stone laid in
this, yes, this prison
was lovingly placed, and
only ever maintained by

myself

freedom is stopping
this unrequited love
this forlorn ache
this lover's sigh

for bricks stacked to build
my prison
and I need not stay

about: fear of freedom

dark pools of ageless, sleepless brown
feel trapped
feel enclosed
feel kept

angular pains
ripping, tearing, burning

out of you through honeyed lips
honeyed tears
honeyed agony

you see the tempest in your heart
the storm in your mind
and long for the freedom of embracing

about: laura who runs

goldenrod colored lace
turned away to show to me
but not look in my eyes

as painfully as you could use me
as used up as I long to be

until the very last drop of who I am disappears
like a mustard seed in the folds of your pillows

happy birthday to us
we got what we wanted

about: toxic relationships

beautiful herald
you aren't all the other things
that prophets are
in robes of old

words on scritta
words emerging from the hive of thoughts
words like a honey harvest

and they are you
in some private place
where words can make things ok

keep speaking and keep
going

about: mary jane

years gone
disappeared back into the darkness
where they first came

my armor diminished
my artifice tarnished, useless

these years never sheltered me
never loved me
never told me it was ok

and now I put to rest these voices
I soothe their wailing accusations
and send them away

about: time wasted

half-finished sketches
smudged pencil lines ending nowhere
thoughts expressed like a radio dancing between stations

a single dowsing rod spinning on invisible axes
telling where the water runs
ran
to tell us where to build the house

the old one is broken
falling
rotten

about: uncertainty of a future life

like a mummified heart
like a shell
like a husk

dry to the touch
crumbles at suggestions
at the will of others

old is how it felt
in that place
that was too young, bloodied

about: myself

silver and black
interlaced and intertwined and interdependent
of victors lines they have clawed up steep
rocks of ages
cleft to no longer hide
but show them
SHOW. THEM.

in the face of the deep
on the peak of the mount
taking shot after shot from false prophets
and sages

about: the election result of 2020

a ghost straining to live again
a mist that wants to be rain
a whispered shout

a mustard seed
a fleeting thought
a train's whine in the dark before dawn

by will alone
fails me
but still leaves a stain
the stain is a warning

that death waits the other way

about: faith

scars look like stitches in wrong places
red welts to hold me together
where I tried to come apart

no pit deep enough to keep the light out
until I realized I was pushing
pulling
straining against the light

because it hurts the corners
where it touches dark
dusty places

about: the pain of self-discovery

no cassandra
heard but unbelieved

all-seeing
and unseen

cursed to know
and be unknown

a chandelier
in an abandoned house
clinking in a wind that

no one feels
no one hears

about: my childhood

blocks of pillow talk
like concrete dividers

will keep us sleeping

afraid to wake up and
know

that it's over but the shouting
and the whimpers

of mourning in the morning
while the night like aromas of
autumn rain and decaying
leaves of leaving

fade

about: fear of divorce

loveless
starving, but unwilling to keep eating poison
parched, but only bile to drink
heartless
a pound, not flesh but stone
a penny, not thoughts but wishes
scared
of endings

and hurt

of no more beginnings

and

life yet to live

about: not knowing what real love is

cling like death to a fantasy
you breathe easy
but

my lungs full
of you

exhale
that I no longer need love
that I no longer breathe that toxic gas
that I know what evil lurks in this heart

that you would show
me patience and truth

until I can't
breathe

about: dying to myself

it's all crows flying west

that book was me
wrist deep in a puppet
throwing my voice

lil Paul the Apostle
that movie with Hannibal and a black beard
where they found that girl, that little girl
most likely of color

they said she speaks to demons
but you ain't

about: the demoniac girl part one

know when she met that
demon it was
her father selling her as a fortune
tell her, yes you tell her, why you think
you know who you are
but never quite known
impressive and imperiled

and so she pointed hands
forced down
as her master raped her

pointed fingers and said

about: the demoniac girl part two

THEY SERVE THE MOST HIGH
she... I.... scream to be known
day and night she screamed

for him lil Paul the Apostle
to see her
to free her

let the reader understand
until I see her, I'll never free her
...
selah
...
i'll cast her
aside but also in silver
so that I... oh I would always
overshadow myself in the glint of
a mirror have I been

about: the demoniac girl part three

susurration, wind aflutter
eyes through glass, as liquid refracts

through damp kittens' prints
on a cold kitchen floor

we only see each other as
future reflections

about: thinking of a friend

no hole deep enough for shame
no horizon close enough for hope
no arms strong enough to lift
no hearts soft enough for grace

sparks, like a blink in the dark
say maybe
and please

as a future dances in shadows

about: fear of not knowing myself

tears of anger, forbidden
smile

welts, hot and pulsing
smile

forgiveness, enforced
smile

be nothing, no one
smile

these scars, how did they get here
smile

about: childhood where emotions were forbidden

the shell is a

dirty alleyway
police cars flowing by
either end
dopplers of sirens

the smell of fresh graffiti
under a gray sky
filled with trash

no one is there
lonely garbage

about: my heart, as an empty alley

old wooden handle
scratched smooth by years
of using

it's no use

how many hands have laid on you
twisting, turning, using

soothing the ache
to make happy, to fix
to see the smile
la petite mort
death, even, using

but now cracked
but now splintered
retired
what is your use

about: my vices

untethered on the open sea
weeping waves, weeping bow, weep

firsts, seminal tears
soaked in the effluence of soul

choking, constricted
gasping for air

leaving whispers

about: uncertainty from revelation

you caught a laugh
there like a spider, silver, spinning
the web around you that
captures, entangles, and gently

cradles

laughs, tears, sighs, butterflies, colored stage lights, warmth in the dark, and

the little breezes fluffed by angels lifting off
with a silver tinkle.

about: crystal

the word deserve
is poison on my lips

when life is death
the bridge is out but there's no sign

warning, flashing, for decades

faust's offer, the price too high

about: letting go of old ways

disappointment painted a murky grey-brown
across the door to imaginary freedom

coloring it in filth

freedom can't be real
but death is

about: bitterness

cardboard sword and tinfoil shield
won't fix the deeper aches

the bruised and bitten heel
the needle tears a hole

golden plaque for your addiction
dirty penny for your shoe

walking on bloody feet
making it "worth it"

you burned your heart out
because mommy didn't love you

about: codependency

that tip of nauseous adrenaline
coating the apple-flavored taboo

waiting for me
glistening in summer sun
with bright darkness and sweaty heat

demanding, enticing, panting, and heaving
into my lungs
reaper's dusty breath

about: temptation

my heart considered itself
insatiable
untethered

my pride climbed a mountain to feel tall

my fists clenched sand to keep it in the flood

esau, my great father
jezebel, my great mother
zedekiah son of kenaanah, my great brother

in tears and blood, i might be a child again

about: anger at myself

feather in the canyon breeze
caresses the slopes of stone

not withered, not dry
just waiting for the rain that comes
in time

thorns, but gently, glide across
the face, telling of a fountain
deep

about: sarah part one

she said, "you don't know the road you'll have to walk" and she was right
this oft-wrong oracle was more than right

but who could have known the miles and tears
the lives created
the lives left in dusty deserts

and now the threads overlap and threaten to noose
to garrote

about: my mother

tinkling chimes
a stake in the ground
the smell of fresh earth

you were scared
because you didn't know what was next
the feel of a screen door under your fingertips

you hadn't seen them fight
you were sweating in the humidity
and nothing was the same

about: a child of divorce

the plucking of the strings
spaces where they cross
spaces where they merge and braid

into time and the unavoidable
creaking and groaning as they rub coarse wires

to hear these melodies is madness
but it can't be that

it can't be

and must be

about: a universe of possibilities

like threads, your heart is a weave of gentle murmurs
calling out, but never above a whisper

in obscurity, in the corner
where two walls shield you from behind

the arrows left their marks in your soul
and you swore never again

but again is all you have
until

about: a different sarah

everything is a broken mirror
where you shame and hate and sneer at who looks back

insatiable hunger to see someone, anyone else

as judge
as prosecution

convicted of failures to be someone else
unable to know yourself
unwilling to love yourself

as regent on high, you judge

about: hating myself

i dance on lines of fate
pulled taught through aged fingers

plucking, humming, building, building
as my feet glide across ages

this life and all of my others
my multitudes of choices and sighs and mistakes

plinking into an eternity where this song
is sung in the dark

about: what ifs

the sound of an eggshell, cracking
the sound of a dry leaf

as you turn under the weight of the wheel
as time remembers the years of silence

you whip from reality to reality
your tears scattering

tears that are, and tears yet to be
will land like ink on pages

about: laura who runs

not too close
you assure the world

collapsing back, retreating, withdrawing
until you can barely see the horizon anymore

wrapping in sweaters against a cold
that is more inside than out

framed in gold
held in stasis

waiting to be seen

about: country laura

i draw your face with words
tracing lines with gentle murmurs

i bend the river with flowery language
to show you my strength

you flit, by seconds, from hand to hand
but not yet mine

between lines of life, death, and ennui
i wait to feel you land

about: writing poems about my friends

undiluted
but you hear "you are," from just behind

like smoke where nothing is burning
and you wince

every time is the last time
every fight is the last fight
every wince is the last one

your fear paints you
your rejection has scarred you
but you are not less, not undiluted

about: jolene

like springs coiled, fragile, tinking
afraid you'll snap if tugged

seeds in your hand are never planted
words in your heart are never shared

push them into good soil
and live life

about: fear

silent pauses betray guilty thoughts
swept up and swept away
your fantasy needs time
your confidence needs suffering

let the incense of your frustration rise
in groans and sighs

your eyes younger than your soul, looking up into
heat and light of a world you don't understand

about: childhood

you brace and hear the hemp rope groan
but nothing is there

in autumn colors you feel strong
oranges and browns flowing near to your bones

shoes feel heavy like grey skies
heart full of warmth and anxiety

because you can't say no

about: jessica

porcelain, laced with cracks
holding curved tensions, like

brutish intentions to end you
only concentrated your essence

and you haven't wasted it
you aren't done

but with streams of tangled thoughts
you ascend into strength

about: trish

marble telamon cracked, splintering
shaking arms

how heavy the words atop your shoulders
that death would wait

but not for you
maiming, draining, leaving

but not for you
as you collapse alone

facing what you knew would come
lifting grief into heaven

about: perseverance

like a trudging vampire at sup
not to immortals fount
but to a youth ripped from grasp

like a wolf in winter to red snow
not to survive coldest wind
but to feed a long dead fire

like a lying mirror's sinful glance
not to primp or preen
but to remember, to taste, to shudder

about: craving youth

it was a chase before i knew it
and that wasn't fair
and you know it
because i'm no rabbit dashing
no sprint in my feet
no flight in my legs
no wings churning from my spine

       you knew i was just caught
       seized
       and it wasn't fair

about: fear and panic

you desire it from my lips
to absolve you from blue guilt, saying it yourself

you want red betrayal to have been worth it
his fall to be your rise

a crumb of cake, a winking eye
crossing through what you could only write in purple

but never speak

about: a person who wounded and almost killed me part one

your thorns taste sweet
your innocence is rancid

twirled, embraced, stuck fast in the gasp
you haven't forgotten

it's never your fault
through layers of baby talk

and still
name me when the years are gone
and the hurt remains like crackling, seared remains

about: a person who wounded and almost killed me part two

embers trapped in alabaster
glowing through cracks with furious glory

you blaze against
you cast sparks

with passion you chase
with fire you consume

strength belied by fragility
knowing you gave up one for the other

may you burn forever

about: auburn

i named you, drunken, pacing gravel, barefoot

I knew you then, I know you now

the moon over the hills that night as someone else confessed my sin

i said your name because I felt safe

shame endures like moonlight dew

about: that night

my hands and the trouble
they brought these agile
servants, quick to falter

about: being tired of myself

selah

about: taking a moment to put your own poem on this page

every thread of possible
laid bare before me
in the light of a christmas candle
sputtering its wick coughs and its flame sighs,

there was christmas 2003,
when we should have danced, the two of us,
in only the light of the christmas tree,
with no music but the sound of carolers who were coming down the street,

there was the christmas of 2018,
when we should have met outside that cooking store,
with you holding a wrapped spatula,
and you smiled and disarmed me with no apology for your gift,

there was our first christmas of 2021,
when you stepped off the plane for the last time,
and we'd be together forever a second time,
but you were sheepish about how your hair looked from the flight,

who could forget 2006,
when you were on that date with him,
and he was pretending to love you,
while we made eyes all night at that party,

about: meet-cute part one

these memories twinkle like those lights you love and hate,
in reflections of those dangerous glass globes that we hang with flimsy wires,
where and when we should have been,
and how christmas has never quite made us laugh or cry,

do you think of me?
as we lay in separate worlds, in separate weaves of the cloth,
as separate lives never once intersecting,
and count another could have christmas.

about: meet-cute part two

the space between blanket and mattress, in winter
where feet probe about to feel the familiar foot of another
dangling in horizontal limbo
hoping to find a match,

air snatching warmth from a nose peeking out over the comforter
the cold is crisp and quiet
breathing is slow and labored with rest
never wanting to leave the warm embrace,

weighted down like i'm made lighter than air,
when it's so obvious i would dig a hole and disappear into it
should that option become available,

tangled up for comfortable
sighs not meant to entice nor engage
just a sound of comfortable repose
where being there is all of it.

about: cold nights under covers

like a caricature of a used cars salesman
down on his luck
up on his doubts

i scrawl
and scrawl
plans on torn up, greasy napkins
how to save
how to escape
how to make it okay again

like tattooing a dead body
with makeup
and gentle sprays of cheap perfume
hoping i'll love her

love is no bargain
nor is it a pure sacrifice
but some commingling of smoke and
mirrors that need a polish and need a shine
and need to be broken for more than 7 years ago

i reach to the bottom
i scoop through the layers of detritus and memories
hoping to find it
a lost ring

about: the cost of love

that door
to that house party deep

inside

my mind

that door doesn't creak
but it blows

open

wide

and joy and scandal and rumors yet to come
come tumbling out with
clouds

and

shrieks
and delights
of an 80s movie house party
and don't tell me
why that's wrong
because i don't care

about: where my poetry comes from

I called this book SHORT BLUES because between September and December I experienced my whole life turning inside out. I cataloged the people and the places and the feelings with these short poems, on the blue bird website, Twitter.

These have been short, blue chirps in the dark with all of you. Staring at your phones, or reading on your computer or tablet, you were all there for it.

And now it's done.

Thank you for being here.

Love,
Gabriel

about: the end of this little poetry book

CPSIA information can be obtained
at www.ICGtesting.com
Printed in the USA
BVHW011211040321
601714BV00011B/705